silence

Jerome W. Berryman

Illustrated by Lois Kilberg

silence

CHURCH
PUBLISHING
INCORPORATED

Church Publishing
19 East 34th Street
New York, NY 10016
www.churchpublishing.org

Cover design and typesetting by Beth Oberholtzer

Library of Congress Cataloging-in-Publication Data
A record of this book is available from the Library of Congress.

ISBN-13: 9781640652958 (paperback)

To Coleen Berryman, who has joined her Mom, Thea.
Now I have two guardian angels.

I walked between two trees.
It was like a door.

A path appeared
on the forest floor,
so I took a step.

It was quiet.
No trains, cars, trucks,
airplanes, or loud talk
hurt my ears.

I took another step.

It was still.
No breeze, leaves,
squirrels, trees, birds,
or worms moved.

I took one more step,
then stopped.

A box blocked the path.
It was old, like dirt and rocks.
A curving "S" was cut into the lid.
It hushed me through and through.

I knelt down and opened the box, but there was nothing inside to see, hear, touch, taste, or smell. Something else was there.

I took away the sides
and put them by the path.
I took away the bottom and
put it in the grass.
Now only what was left
was there to know.

It moved, so
I moved too,
crawling
on my hands and knees
until it stopped once more.

I lay down
to wonder, and
came so close
that we smiled
the same smile.
It was so wide
we went inside
what has no outside.

All began to fade.
Even my words
wandered away.
Where they went
I do not know.

When my words
came back,
they were alive
with the light
of the First Day.

Now I could see
something new,
and I knew how
to say it.

As I walked back
along the path,
the feeling grew
that God was there,
like air to breathe.
It was odd, but
I knew what I knew.

I wonder what silence could really be . . .

I wonder where it comes from . . .

I wonder where it goes . . .

I wonder if it's big or small . . .

I wonder if it's old or always new . . .

I wonder where you are in silence . . .

I wonder where silence is in you . . .

I wonder what has no outside . . .